The Book of
EXCELLENCE

ॐ

The Book of
EXCELLENCE

236 HABITS
OF EFFECTIVE
SALES PEOPLE

Byrd Baggett

INSIGNIS, CORP.
Nashville, Tennessee

Published in Nashville, Tennessee, by Rutledge Hill Press, 211 Seventh Avenue North, Nashville, Tennessee 37219.

Typography by D&T / Bailey Typesetting, Nashville, Tennessee
Design by Bruce Gore, Gore Studio

Library of Congress Cataloging-in-Publication Data

Baggett, Byrd.
   The book of excellence: 236 habits of effective sales people/
Byrd Baggett.
   p.   cm.
 ISBN 1-55853-171-8
 1. Selling — Quotations, maxims, etc. I. Title
HF5438.25.B27   1992
658.8'5 — dc20   92-5897
                                                    CIP

Printed in the United States of America
      1 2 3 4 5 6 7 8 9 — 97 96

In loving memory of

My loving mother
Coach Cleburne Price
My dear friend, Hank Eddins

Special thanks to Jeanne,
my wife and best friend.
Her faith has been a blessing in my life.

Introduction

I NEVER PLANNED to write a book.

I'm a salesman, and by nature I'm a man of action. For eighteen years I have pounded the streets and have managed sales staffs in the office furniture and consumer products industries.

And so it came as quite a surprise to realize that a simple exercise I had done for my own benefit was growing into a book. I had begun a list of habits that produce success, and soon what had been started almost as a lark became an exciting adventure. When I showed my list to friends, several wanted copies of their own. And when I showed it to a successful sales and marketing consultant, he advised me to look for a publisher. "The sales profession needs to get back to the basics," he stated.

I agreed with him. I had begun the list following yet another boring training seminar that was long on theory but short on reality. I've learned that very little of what is in the seminars, books, cassettes, videos, and study guides is of practical use. Very little of it results in increased sales and profits.

Partly out of frustration and partly as an adventure, I asked myself what eighteen years of sales experience had taught me. Soon I was writing. And soon I had filled several pages with insights that I am confident will make a winner of every salesperson who applies them consistently.

The Book of Excellence is what I have learned from observing the top performers in many fields. This not only includes conventional sales professionals, but also bankers, accountants, lawyers, doctors, stock brokers, and others. I believe passionately that these women and men have achieved their success by keeping it simple and by developing positive habits.

There are no page numbers here, so start and end where you want. Most importantly, remember that you don't have to be a rocket scientist or a brain surgeon to be successful in sales. Here is what I have learned about the habits that bring success in this profession I love so much.

–Byrd Baggett

The Book of
EXCELLENCE

∾

Excellence
is not
optional.

 formin

The nineties will see
the death of the order taker.
Are you an order taker?

Proper planning
prevents poor performance.
Remember this as the five Ps.

℘

Success at the
expense of faith and family
really is failure.

Be a team player.
Prima donnas don't last.

છ

A good marketing plan
without sales and profits is a
guaranteed failure. Don't get the
cart before the horse.

True wisdom
is not a fad.

∽

Participate in a lead-sharing
group. Suggested members:
accountant, lawyer, developer,
architect, telecommunications
representative, marketing expert
from your local chamber of
commerce. This group will keep
you in the know.

Develop a sense
of urgency to your work
and pay attention to details.

ॐ

Know your market.
Where is the business?
Who has it?

Don't put
all your eggs (time)
into one client's basket.

&

Make at least
one new account call
per week.

Always ask for
the order!
Don't worry about
your technique or style.

℘

Plan your sales calls
a minimum of one week
in advance.

The customer's
perception *is* reality.

ॐ

Customers will find a way
to buy from you if they like you.
They will also find a way not
to buy from you if they
don't like you.

Know where your sales increases will come from. They won't just happen!

&

Always have five new target accounts in development.

Have a single,
consolidated planning calendar
that you keep with you at
all times.

୧୬

Never be too busy
to follow up on the
small things.

Manipulating outcomes
never provides the
best results.

෨

A bad attitude
cancels all other
positive skills.

Be present mentally
as well as physically
at meetings.

ری

Concentrate on your job,
not on everyone else's.

Be as critical of yourself
as you are of others.

❧

Good looks are
truly only skin deep.
Performance is lasting.

Are you
becoming complacent?

℘

Arrogance is deadly.

Do you add value
to your customer's business?

೪೨

Always carry
an adequate supply
of business cards.

You're not learning
anything when you're talking.

 හ

Timing is everything.
Let it happen naturally.

Each day
you get better or worse.
It's your choice.

ↄ

Know your
clients' hobbies.

Send birthday
and anniversary cards.

೮

Push yourself.
Only you can motivate you.

Be a part of excellence,
not critical of it.

છ

Don't be late
for an appointment.
It's all right for customers
to be late.

Be open to change.

✌

Carry an adequate supply of change. You never know when you will need to feed the parking meter or use a pay telephone.

Believe in yourself,
your company, your products.

&

Spend a minimum of
four hours per day
in front of customers.

Watch your weight.

ↄ

Do your socks
match your suit? Don't wear
light socks with dark suits.

God has given you
another day.
Rejoice and be thankful!

భs

Become actively
involved in your community
through a civic club.

B eware of those who drop in.
They are time wasters.

ℰ

C ustomers love
humility.

Opportunities come
in unexpected packages.

❧

Don't wear
too much jewelry.

Be yourself.
You can't fool
the audience!

❧

Great potential is
one of life's heaviest
burdens.

Be nice.

∽

Watch your jokes.
Make sure they are
wholesome and appropriate
for the audience.

Don't get trapped
at the purchasing agent level.
Start at the top before
progressing to the purchasing
department.

୧

Keep
your competitors
on their toes!

The best defense
is still a good offense.

తు

Are there any sales
training manuals, programs,
books, or cassettes collecting
dust on your shelves? Why?
You can still learn from them.

Be committed to your faith,
your family, and your company
–in that order.

❧

Send your customers
plants or flowers on
special occasions.

Resist fads,
whether in clothes
or language.

ᔐ

Send your clients
copies of news articles
in which you believe
they have an interest.

Are your
shoes polished?

&

Does your belt
match your shoes?

Get up early
and work late.

ↄ

Ask your customers
to audit your performance.
Their opinion is the only one
that truly matters.

Tell
the truth!

∾

Are you doing
the same things this year
that you did last year?
If so, you are
losing ground.

Be well manicured.

ᏟᎧ

Breakfast appointments
create sales opportunities.
Clients tend to be fresh and
more receptive then.

Follow the leader,
not the follower.

෮ঌ

It is very important
that you like yourself.

Plan the following week
by this Friday.

ᏋᎧ

Look at life through the
windshield, not through
the rear-view mirror.

Set your watch ahead
five minutes. You will be
on time and will
experience less stress.

❧

Don't waste
your energy on
negative gossip.

Expect excellence
from yourself and
from others.

~

Be serious
about your business.

Have fun and
celebrate your successes.

❧

Check the Help Wanted
section. This will help you
identify the most progressive
companies. They always are
excellent sales leads.

Give business leads
to professional associates.
Most likely they will
return the favor.

❧

Call someone you
haven't seen for a while.
Don't just think about
doing it.

Never take your business relationships for granted.

ରେ

Use all the resources available to you. Solo performers have a limited range!

Be loyal
to your employer.

ↄ

A customer's
opinion is formed
within the first five minutes
after you meet.

Have a professional, but not necessarily expensive, wardrobe.

જી

If you consistently have to be the cheapest to get the order, you are not a professional salesperson.

Work harder *and* smarter.

ε৯

Reserve the middle
of the day and luncheons
for your clients.

Monday mornings
and Friday afternoons
should be work time,
not wasted time.

ფ

Write it down.
Don't rely on
your memory.

Seek advice
from successful people.

෯

Expect others to
make appointments with you.
Your time is important.

If possible,
return calls within
one hour.

❧

Do you add enough value
to more than compensate
for the difference you charge
over your competitor's
lower price?

Be a student of your
industry: trends, competition,
niche opportunities.

❧

Ask questions
and identify needs before
you present solutions.

Underpromise
and overperform.

ɞ

If you follow up,
you will be a hero.

Knowledge
without application
is useless.

&

There is a
wealth of opportunity
for the true sales professional
in today's economy.

Listen.
Listen. Listen.

 co

Develop relationships with
people at various decision-
making levels within your
accounts. Personnel
changes are inevitable.

Don't compete
with your customers.

ↄ৩

Rapport is not developed
on the telephone. Face-to-face
interaction develops long-term
business relationships.

Choose effectiveness
over efficiency.

◆

Don't go just for
the big hit. The greatest
opportunites exist in small-
to medium-size companies.

Ask your customers
for sales leads.

෫ඁ

The top 20 percent of sales
producers earn sixteen times
more income than the
bottom 80 percent.

Don't just talk
about it, do it!

❧

Watch those buzzwords!
They probably do not mean
the same to your clients as
they do to you.

Excellence
knows no time clock.

℘

Rely on your support staff.
Your time should be spent
in front of the customer,
not in the office.

Spend two hours at home per week in creative thinking, planning, and working on sales appointments.

෮

Motivation is what turns knowledge and skill into success.

If you were your
own competitor, how would you
win over your accounts?

છ૭

Be a strong number two
at your competitors' accounts.

Always concentrate
on developing new business.
You never know when or how
you will lose one of
your key accounts.

෬

Don't leave
an opening for competition.

Technology is
not a replacement
for hard work.

ↄↄ

Do your clothes
or breath reek of
smoke? Your customers
will find this offensive.

All play
and no work
does not work.

ՀՅ

When you work
hard, you have earned
the right to play.

Don't slack up after a big sale. Turn it up another notch.

℘

Does your company consider you profit or overhead? Hope it's not the latter!

Emulate the
habits of the winners,
not the also-rans.

෫ඁ

Make sure your customers
know your product and service
capabilities. It's amazing
how many do not.

Strive to make
yourself and your company
number one.

⁊

Solicit feedback
from your competitors' accounts.
This is very useful for
identifying ways to
penetrate them.

Set goals.
Monitor your status on a
quarterly basis. Modify
your actions accordingly.

ᴈ

Never say negative
things about your company
to your clients. Instead,
communicate your concerns
to your management.

Don't handle administrative duties during prime selling time.

ↄ৲

Establish an exercise routine. This is important to your mental well-being.

You have a choice
between developing good habits
and developing bad habits.

❧

Carry your business
card file. You never
know when you will need
a telephone number.

Don't let your
ego get in the way.

త

Carry an adequate supply
of cash. Restaurants don't
always take credit cards,
and it is embarrassing to ask
your customer to pay.

"He who sows sparingly
will also reap sparingly,
and he who sows bountifully
will also reap bountifully."
2 Corinthians 9:6

❧

Is your hair
shaggy and unruly?
Is it too long? Do you use
too much hair spray?

Send a plant to
your customer's open house.
It still works.

∽

Dress conservatively.
It still conveys an image of
dependability and
responsibility.

Are your clothes
losing their crispness?

ɛっ

Watch the amount
of liquor you consume.
Your credibility could be lost
in one evening.

Tell your vendors who
behave professionally how much
you appreciate them.

&

Take an active,
not passive, role in
helping your community.

Observe five
habits of a
successful salesperson
you know.

 handle

Don't spend your time
worrying about why you
can't win an account.
Concentrate your thoughts
on how you *can* win it.

If you are a veteran,
learn from the rookies.

જી

Use a beeper.
That will let the office
get in touch with you
when a customer needs you
in an emergency.

Silence
is a necessity,
not a negative.

⁓

What percentage of your
customers' total business
are you receiving?

Don't
confuse efforts
with results.

&

Are you presenting
new ideas or concepts to
your clients? If not, your
competition will and
you will lose.

Keep sharpening your
written communication skills.

&

Avoid "canned" presentations.
They are boring.

Don't talk down
to your customers.

∾

Make two morning
and two afternoon appointments
your minimum daily goal.

Measure three times,
cut once.

ᑫ

Sell your customers
what they want, not what
you *think* they need.

Do you thoroughly know
the features and benefits
of your products?

❧

Don't give away
the farm!

Check your breath before
you meet your customers.

∽

When you start
taking your customers
for granted, you start
losing them.

Don't wear cheap cologne
or perfume. And don't use
an overpowering amount.

∽

Let your support
staff know how special
and important they are.
Be sincere when you tell them!

Do you feel
the customer is fortunate
to do business with you?
You better not!

ɕ৲

Remember, it is
harder to keep an account
than it was to get it.

$$B_e\ nice$$
to secretaries.

℘

$$D_o\ you\ create\ sales$$
opportunities or just
react to them?

Proofread all
correspondence!

๛

Reserve a weekly
luncheon or breakfast for
your spouse and children.
This time will be more
important to them than
your business successes.

Make appointments.
Remember, your client's time
is very important.

છ

Much potential business
and better profit opportunities
exist in rural areas
because most of your competitors
stay in cities.

Take time
to sharpen your saw.

❧

Don't expect
prime accounts to
be handed to you.
Be proactive and develop
new business.

Participate in
a fellowship group.

❧

Don't expect your
customers to tell you
they are unhappy with
your level of service.

Be consistently
persistent, but
not a pest.

ↄ

Do what you said
you were going to do,
when you said you were going to
do it, and how you said you
were going to do it.

Strive for
increases in profits,
not just sales volume.

❧

It's not the big
things you do for your
clients that make you successful.
It's the small things.

Spend as much time
providing customer service
as you do talking about it.

❧

Sales is not for everyone.
Don't feel you are a failure
if you try this profession
and it doesn't fit you.

Know how
your products differ
from those of your competitors.

ဗာ

Invest your
time in learning,
not just in training.

Stop, listen, and think before you respond.

೮ง

Develop and commit to memory ten questions that will help you identify a customer's needs.

If you're not changing,
you're not in first place.

෯

Smile.
Customers like
positive people.

When you are out of the office
call for messages at 10:00 A.M.,
2:00 P.M., and 4:00 P.M.

છ

Aim high.
You normally hit
what you aim for.

Relationships
require more than
one sales call.

ℰℬ

Target accounts that fit
your profile for the
optimum customer.

Don't tell
your customers how good
you are. Show them!

∾

Your chances
for success increase in
proportion to the number of
sales calls you make.

Be concerned when you lose, but never feel defeated.

Don't dump all your products on your clients. Identify their primary needs and submit your solutions.

Have an objective for
each sales call.

ᏋᏃ

Read *Living Above
the Level of Mediocrity*
by Chuck Swindoll.
(Word, 1987)

Make that extra call
at 4:30 P.M.

ભ

Make a stop in the
bathroom before your
presentation.
This is an excellent time
to check your breath,
teeth, hair and shoulders
for dandruff.

A nice car is
not the key to success.
The key is the driver.

෨

Invest your time in customers
who have the financial ability
to purchase your products
or services.

Your time budget
is as important as your
financial budget.

෬

What's your best remedy
when you are feeling down?
Try making several new sales
calls. You will be amazed
at the results.

Never accept mediocrity.

❧

Be consistently
aware of how you are
utilizing your time.
Conduct monthly audits.

Take time
to recharge your batteries.
Rest is important.

Ↄↄ

Improve your
speaking skills by enrolling in
Toastmasters or by attending a
Dale Carnegie course.

Mend broken relationships.
Negative energy will keep you
from being productive.

ॐ

If you want to impress your
customers, make written notes
when they respond to
your questions.

Congratulate your peers
on their accomplishments.

ૐ

Thank your
spouse for his or her
help and support.

Patience is a virtue.
Don't give up!

તજ

Invite your customers
out for a glass of iced tea or
lemonade. You will be amazed
at how much they enjoy
the simple pleasures.

Do not be
an underachiever.

෴

Schedule daily quiet
time for planning, relaxing,
and brainstorming.

Always keep social and
business relationships separate.

∽

Concentrate on sales,
not on marketing.

Believe in yourself.
If you don't, who will?

෨෩

Be aggressive,
but not oppressive!

If you smoke, don't light up
in front of your customers.

❧

Keep your car,
especially the interior,
clean at all times.

Move fast.

❧

Remember that
none of us is more important
than the team.

Don't be
too comfortable.

ↄ

Sales is like banking.
You have to make the deposits
before you can participate
in the withdrawals.

Don't waste your
time on conceptual training.
Be practical.

↭

Don't keep doing the
wrong things over and over.
Learn from your mistakes
and take another approach.

Ask for help.

∽

Hold annual
feedback sessions with
your customers. You will be
amazed at the benefits.

There is no
replacement for effort.

&

If you can't find the time
to do it right the first time,
how will you find the time
to do it over and over?

Success does not come easily. Are you willing to pay the price?

❧

Excellence usually takes a little longer.